# Power Carving
# Santas with Tom Wolfe

Text written with and
photography by
Jeffrey B. Snyder

Schiffer Publishing Ltd

77 Lower Valley Road, Atglen, PA  19310

# ACKNOWLEDGMENTS

I would like to thank the following suppliers for their help: Smoky Mountain Woodcarvers Supply, Inc., P.O. Box 82, Townsend, TN 37882 and Woodcraft Supply Corp., P.O. Box 1686, Parkersburg, WV 26102-1686

Printed in China

ISBN: 0-88740-963-6

**Library of Congress Cataloging-in-Publication Data**

Wolfe, Tom (Tom James)
    Power carving Santas with Tom Wolfe/text written with and photography by Jeffrey B. Snyder.
        p. cm.
    ISBN 0-88740-963-6 (paper)
    1. Wood-carving. 2. Power tools. 3. Wood-carved figurines. 4. Santa Claus in art. I. Snyder, Jeffrey B. II. Title.
TT199.7.W6429    1997
736'.4--dc20                         96-31762
                                     CIP

Published by Schiffer Publishing, Ltd.
77 Lower Valley Road
Atglen, PA 19310
Phone: (610) 593-1777
Fax: (610) 593-2002
Please write for a free catalog.
This book may be purchased from the publisher.
Please include $2.95 for shipping.
Try your bookstore first.

We are interested in hearing from authors with book ideas on related subjects.

# CONTENTS

# INTRODUCTION

After the big Christmas flight, while elves are busy updating the naughty and nice list or planning next year's product lines, what does the jolly old elf do with his spare time? I have been considering the possibilities and have come up with a variety of pastimes Santa might pick up on his days off. Some of Santa's activities have been set in motion, combining Santa and a whirligig. In one of the whirligigs, Santa experiments with a new delivery system, replacing reindeer and sleigh with a biplane.

In the carving project presented, Santa has kicked off the boots, pulled up his favorite chair, and is channel surfing through the polar programming on his TV. You might like to add to this "Surfin' Santa" by including the TV and Mrs. Claus standing in front of it, objecting the Santa's choice in programs.

This project has its challenges. It is carved as a single 7 3/4" x 6 1/2" butternut block. Santa, his chair, and his channel changing "surf board" are all carved together. While this requires more work from the carver (and you can carve the pieces separately if you really want to), these single piece carvings are the ones serious carvers win contests with. Besides, anyone who has been up late on Christmas eve struggling to put together that last gift will appreciate the fact that there is "no assembly required" with this carving method.

Patterns have been provided for six different Santa's, two of which are whirligigs, and one Rudolph. Now, put aside your channel changer, get out of that chair, and let's get busy carving Santa with power tools!

# SURFIN' SANTA

# TOOLS AND PATTERNS

The power tools used to carve the "Surfin' Santa" include a bandsaw to cut out the blank, a power reciprocating chisel (I use a Ryobi, although the Automac is also a fine tool I have used many times) with spring steel chisel blades called Flexcut Carving Tools, a High Tech hand tool (a dental tool) and a flexible shaft Foredom — both fitted with a series of ruby and diamond cutting and grinding burrs in a variety of shapes, a drill press with a Forstner bit, and a small 7/32" eye punch. There are times when only a pocket knife will do. I prefer to use a Case pocket knife. The completed project will be sanded with 200, 300 (or 320) and 400 grit sandpaper.

Although only one side of the pattern is shown here, there *are* two sides to this pattern in this book because the two hands are doing different things. With two patterns you are less likely to forget and leave things out. This figure will all be carved from a single piece of 7 3/4" x 6 1/2" butternut. Butternut is a little expensive but well worth it. The pattern can be shrunk down to fit smaller sized pieces of wood. The chair and Santa can be carved separately. You can basically do whatever you want. This pattern is called the "Surfin' Santa," he's TV surfing with his channel changer.

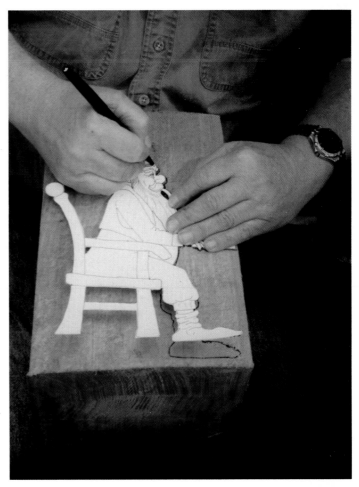

Tracing the outline of the pattern to the block. If you don't get the pattern traced exactly, it doesn't matter. That is part of what makes each carving unique.

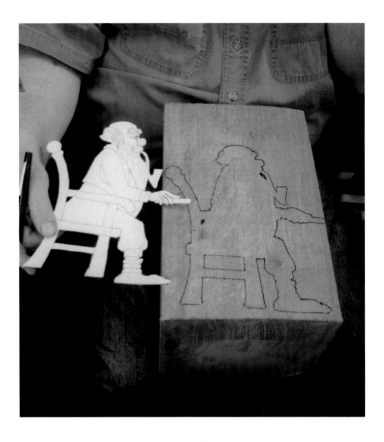

The pattern has been copied to the block.

Mark in the areas which will need to be taken out with a drill. Notice that the pattern does not exactly match the block that was cut out by the bandsaw. A little wood is left over in many places that the saw wouldn't reach. I don't worry about these. With a little extra wood on the nose, for instance, I have the choice of making a little round nose, a hooked nose, or whatever else suits my whim at the moment.

Cut the outline of the pattern out on the bandsaw. As I said, this piece can be done in a number of ways. You can carve the chair and the channel changer separately or you can make the whole thing out of a single piece as I am doing here. If you are entering your piece in competition, you need to carve the entire piece from a single block if you expect to be in serious contention. The piece that I am working on now measures 8" x 5 1/2" wide and 9" tall. You can make it any size you want.

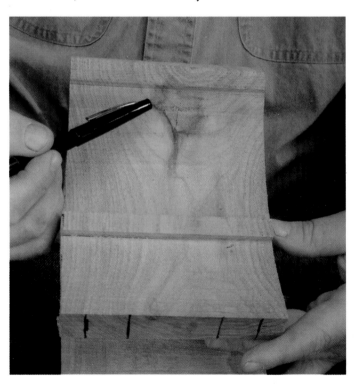

Notice this bad knot in the wood. Find a way to work around these, to place them where they will do the least harm. This one is in the back and I can carve the chair out around it, carving only one standard in back where I might have carved two otherwise.

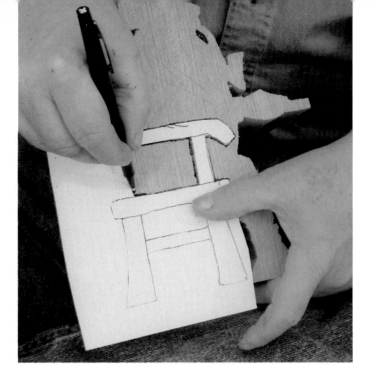

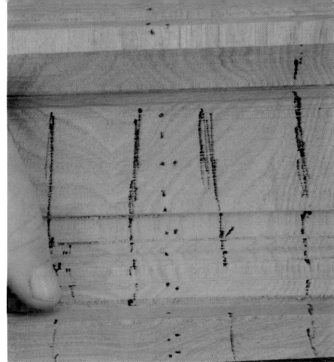

With paper copies of the pattern, you can cut out and trace pieces onto the block to ensure that you do not cut off parts of the block that you need later to finish the piece. Nothing is more aggravating than to realize you have cut off wood needed later for Santa's right arm, his left chair legs, and so on.

I have sketched in the legs and feet on the front view (feet at the bottom where my thumb is). I will need to cut out the excess wood between the legs and on either side of them. For this I am using a drill press.

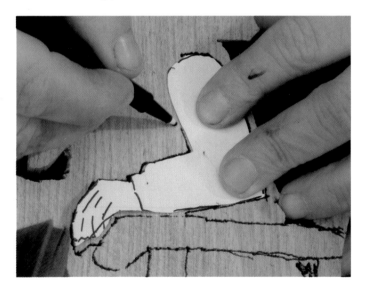

Copying Santa's left arm onto the block to avoid cutting it off.

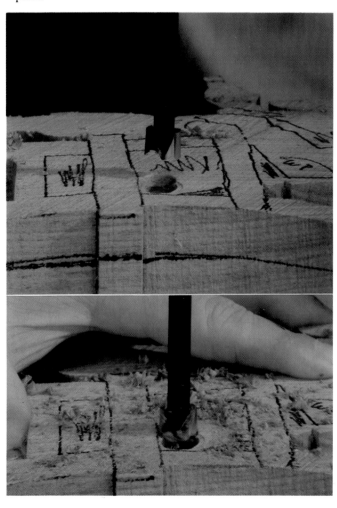

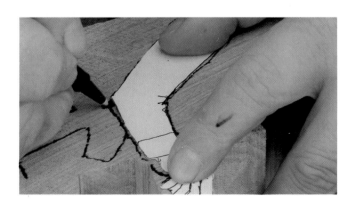

Repeating this process with the right arm.

Using a Forstner bit on the drill press, I'm going to start underneath the arm, removing excess wood down to Santa's seat. The Forstner bit works well at any angle.

The excess wood has been removed down below Santa's arm and the chair arm to the level of the side of his body. Leave a little extra wood on Santa's side, as the Forstner bit leaves a tee-tiny tip from the end of the bit in the flat bottom of the drill hole.

On the rest of the holes drilled, the bit will not get stuck in the hole as each hole overlaps the last one and gives the bit some breathing room.

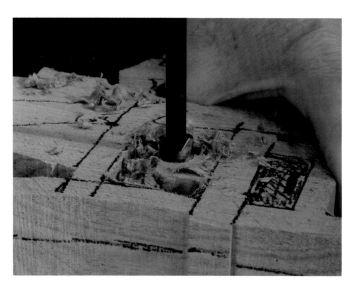

Repeating this process on the other side.

Remove excess wood from the back of the chair between the bottom of the seat and the top of the back chair rung.

The gap between the legs and the back rung is roughed out with the drill press.

Removing the excess wood between the bottom of the seat and the side chair rung. This is a deeply drilled hole. On the first hole drilled the bit may get stuck.

Drill out the gap between the back of the chair and the chair seat. Only drill down as far as the head of the drill bit. That is a good depth at which to locate Santa's "seat."

It is useful to mark off areas in black that you want to cut down with the drill so you don't get confused and take off too much.

As you can see, this bit cuts just as well at an angle as it does straight in. Removing the excess wood from the chair back.

The WP marking stands for "Wide Place." I leave these at the bottom, top, and in several places in the middle of the carving while drilling to keep the piece level on both sides. This keeps the piece stable while I work on it.

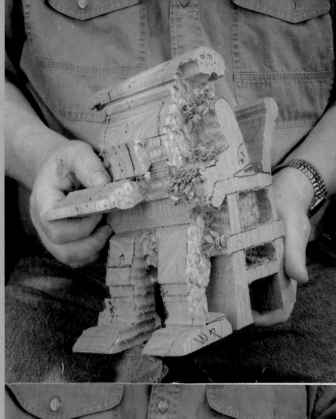

Clean up the rough cut figure with a Ryboli power chisel using a nearly flat chisel blade. The power chisel you can pick up from almost anywhere but the spring steel chisel bits need to be ordered from Smoky Mountain Woodcarvers Supply. These bits are called Flexcut Carving Tools. You need to get the burrs and rough wood cut away to see where you really are before you can start any detailed carving.

Continuing to use the power chisel, angle the carving down from the elbow to the shoulder. The elbows are sticking out.

The figure has been roughed out now with both the band saw and drill press.

Like so.

Removing one of the "Wide Places" down to the outline of Santa's head.

Using a small Foredom flexible shaft power tool with a conical Kutzall burr, remove the excess wood from tight spaces such as this, the area between Santa's arm and the arm of his chair. Experiment with different burr shapes throughout the carving project and find which shapes work best for you in different circumstances.

Removing the extra wood from the outside of the left foot.

The excess wood has been removed with the power chisel. I'm getting the carving down to a square form. From there I will take it down to roughly an octagon shape. After that, I will begin to put in the detail.

There is another tight spot under the arm of the chair where the end of the arm curls down. The Foredom with the conical bit also works well here.

Using the power chisel with a nearly flat chisel blade, cut away the excess wood from the posts of the chair back. Leave enough room at the top to carve balls at the ends of the posts.

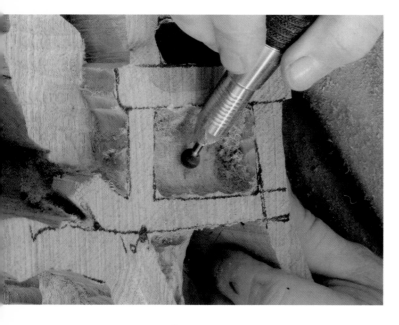

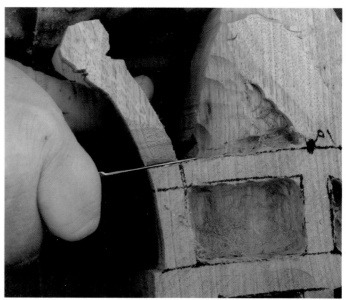

To bring Santa's side down level with the outside of his leg, I'm using the High Tech rotary tool with a ball shaped burr.

Of course, some things are best left to a pocket knife ... a Case knife in this case.

When removing excess wood from the back of the chair, place vertical stop cuts in with the Case knife along the edges of the chair arms, seat bottom, etc. Then notch in at an angle to the stop cut. This clears the way for the power chisel to remove the rest of the excess wood without cutting into pieces you want to keep.

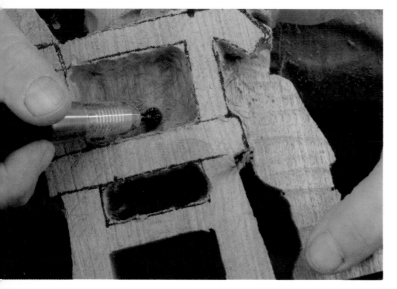

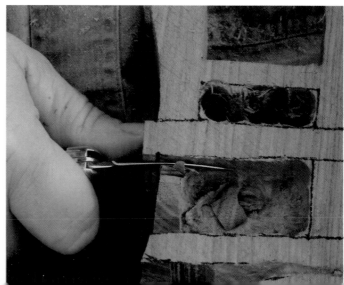

Santa's body is now reduced to the same level as his leg.

Carving back the upper chair post with the power chisel. Carving down to the notch made with the Case knife.

The excess wood has been removed from the chair legs with the power chisel.

Removing excess wood between the chair arm and seat. Working the power chisel between two notches cut with a Case knife keeps the arm and seat safe from being cut away.

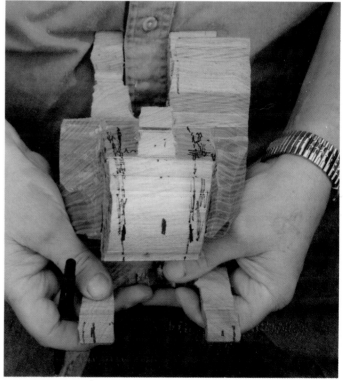

It is time to reduce the size of the head and establish the neck line. Sketch in the outline of the head and beard. I have blackened in areas that need to be cut away.

Put a bit more of a half round chisel head in the power chisel. It removes a little more wood at a time and will work well around the beard and the neck.

Using a near flat chisel head, follow your guide lines and knock down both sides of the head closer to proper proportions.

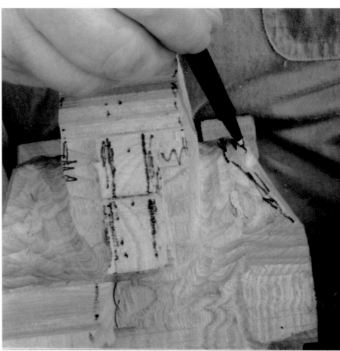

The shoulder comes up a little high. Reduce it until it fits under the hair.

Reducing the shoulder under Santa's hair and defining the edge of his beard.

Things change and you have to keep up with them. As I reduced the head, the shoulders became too broad and square. I will reduce them along the lines marked here with the power chisel and the flatter chisel blade.

Reducing the shoulders.

Work back in to the stop cuts at a 90 degree angle. Remove the excess wood back to the guide lines for the pipe.

Using the same blade in the power chisel, make a series of stop cuts along the edges of the pipe.

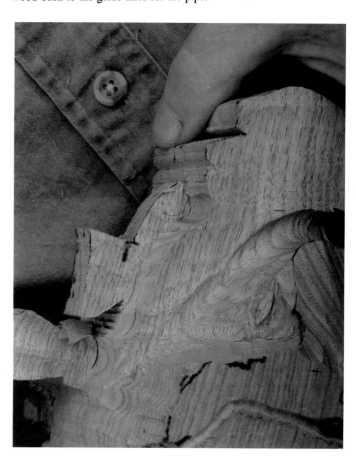

There will be a gap between the curved pipe stem and Santa's chin. Using a half round chisel blade in the power chisel, remove the excess wood away from Santa's chin up to the edge of the pipe stem. The half round will leave a nice curved notch.

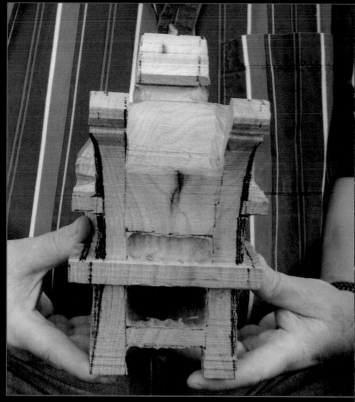

You need to size up the Surfin' Santa as much as possible in the square form. I have drawn in guidelines to follow as I knock off the corners into an octagon shape. I brought in the right arm holding the channel changing "surf board" some. Be careful when moving limbs inward or outward. Move them too far from the pattern position and you will have to adjust the length of the limb. Move the arm in far enough and you will need to shorten it some ... or Santa will have one extra long right arm.

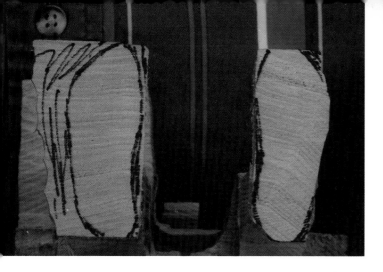

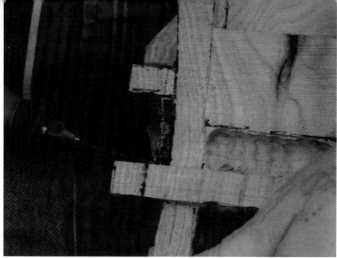

When carving feet, draw in the pattern on the bottoms first. This is an easy way to get them right. Draw in the pattern on the smallest foot first to establish size and then copy that drawing onto the other foot as closely as possible.

Cut down the marked areas along the chair legs with the power chisel and a nearly flat chisel blade. Cut straight down at the edges of the chair seat and arms to create a stop cut line and carve back to the stop cut.

Carve down the feet with a nearly flat chisel blade. If you get the bottoms of the feet down the size the tops will fall into place. These are going to be stocking feet, no shoes required.

Finger measuring: to get the chair leg (or any other feature) down to a standard size, measure along a cut side that is roughly the size you want another side of the leg to be. Use you finger and a pen or pencil to measure and hold that length (your finger lays across the pencil at one edge of the chair leg and the pencil tip reaches to the other edge). Keep you finger at that point along the pencil and lay your finger along the outer edge of the side you wish to mark. The tip of the pencil will come to rest at the proper position. Mark that place. Now both sides can be carved to the same size.

A sharp knife is about the only thing that will get back in here between Santa's backside and the chair. (I don't use any one type of tool all the time.) Round off the corner where Santa and the chair meet. You want his side to stick out about as far as the chair standard (the tall back upright of the chair). This way it will appear, once rounded, that Santa's fat bulges out around the chair.

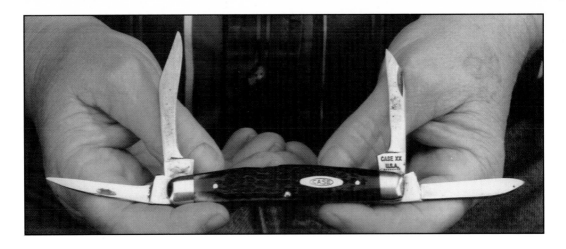

I like the Case Congress style knife with four blades. This large Case gives you a good hand hold. I asked a guy at Case one time why it was called a "Congress." He said that after the Revolution the English wanted to get back into good trade with the U.S. so they gave Congressmen these knives as a good will gesture. However, there is a better story ... it's a Congress because its crooked and the ends are square to wear holes in your pockets just like a congressman will ... a very taxing feature of this knife.

Some areas are very hard to get into. For these you will need to use a long hand chisel and take out the excess wood one little piece at a time.

Using the High Tech with a rough round Kutzall burr to open a space between the back of the arm rest and Santa's back.

Of course, after you've opened things up a bit you may be able to get your Foredom back in there to finish up. You just have to keep trying different things and adjusting the tools you use to what is needed at the moment.

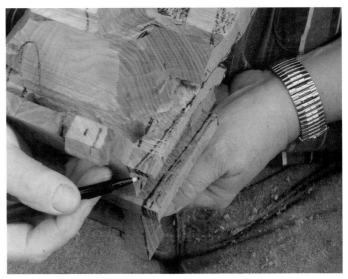

Using the power chisel with a fairly flat blade, narrow the seat and arm rest of the chair toward the back. Chairs are often made that way.

Narrowing the back of the seat.

Reduce the rest of the excess wood from the chair rungs with a nearly flat chisel blade on the power chisel.

The chair rungs need to be reduced. Be careful when reducing these, they are cross-grained. I will use a knife to cut them down to size.

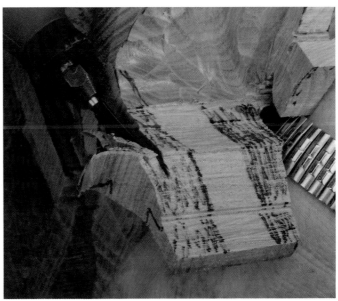

Reduce the arm holding the "surf board" with the power chisel and a nearly flat chisel blade.

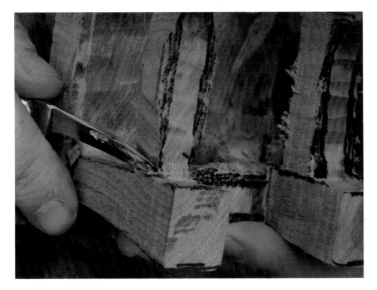

Using a knife, first place stop cuts in the corners where the rungs meet the chair legs. Then cut back to the stop cuts, working the corners down to the reduced rung size.

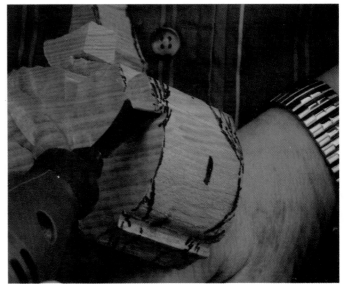

Knocking the sharp corners off the head, creating an octagon shape. I'm using the power chisel with a slightly rounded chisel blade.

Continuing to remove extra wood from the head and face with a nearly flat chisel blade.

Once the stop cuts are in place, remove the rest of the squared edges with the power chisel and a nearly flat blade. Continue this process on all areas of the figure that need to be rounded.

The excess wood has been removed from the head. See the octagon shape?

We're going to round the chair back. Begin by making a stop cut along the line of the chair leg and the back.

Basically, any part of the figure that needs to be rounded, should first be taken from the square shape into the octagon shape by cutting off the sharp corners. For the chair legs, start by making a stop cut along the edge of the chair seat and chair rungs. Cut back at an angle with your knife to these stop cuts.

Cut from near the center of the chair back to the stop cut, sloping downward to create the curve of the back.

The rounded back. I'll just work around this knot and make it part of the piece. It'll give the chair some age.

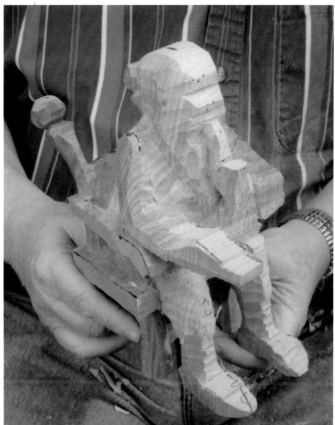

The sharp corners have been removed from this chair leg from top to bottom. Notice the rounded ball on top of the chair leg. Cutting these shapes down to octagons first makes it easier to round them later. As you're knocking off corners, keep your Foredom handy and hollow out areas with excess wood such as where Santa's back meets the chair back and where his elbow is slightly raised off of the chair arm. Use whichever burr best suits you.

Progress. The edges are rounded.

23

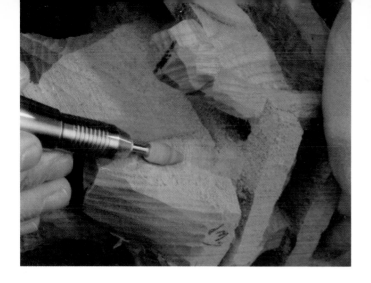

Using the High Tech with a conical burr, hollow out the area between the back of Santa's left arm and his side.

I have hollowed out enough between Santa's left arm and back to define the two. I am now hollowing out between the chair arm and Santa's side.

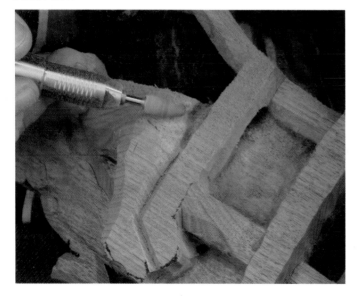

As you are opening things up (hollow them out), begin to round down the figure, taking it from octagon shaped to a more natural rounded shape.

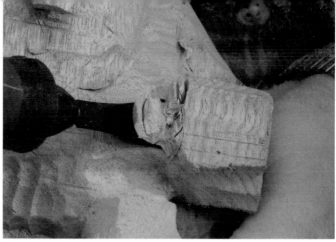

I found a place I overlooked. Use the power chisel with the half round chisel blade to remove wood from between Santa's left hand and his belly. Make a stop cut along the hand first and then angle into the cut from the belly, roughly defining the shape of the jolly old elf's stomach as you go.

The rounded Santa.

Anywhere you know there is going to be an obvious opening, you need to take the High Tech and start that opening before beginning the detail work.

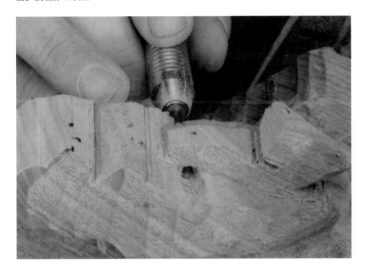

Using a narrow conical burr on the High Tech, undercut the pipe stem where it curves out from the chin. Remember when we notched that area earlier?

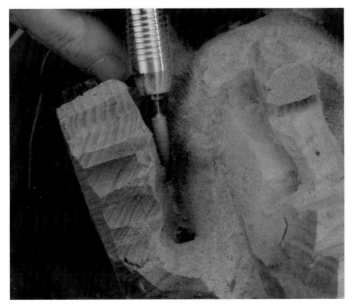

Opening up the area between the left arm and Santa's side using the narrow conical burr.

I have opened up the arms with the Foredom and a long, narrow conical Kutzall burr. From the back you can see that the right arm is crooked, it bows out. I am going to fix that first before doing anything else. This arm is the weakest piece of the figure and I will work on it first and then carve the other arm to match.

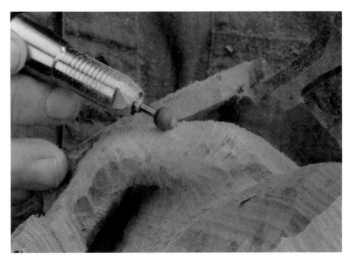

Straightening out the right arm, using the High Tech with a ball shaped burr.

Using the power chisel to bring down the other arm to the rough size that we want. The shoulders were getting a little too wide again. Never cut in one place too long, always keep turning the piece. If you cut too long in one spot, the cutting will get really easy and before you know it you'll have cut in too deep.

Finish undercutting this arm, separating it from the chair arm with the narrow conical burr on the High Tech.

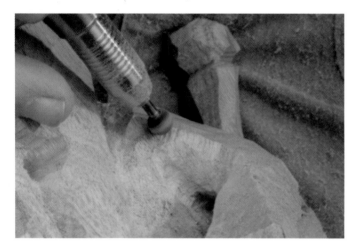

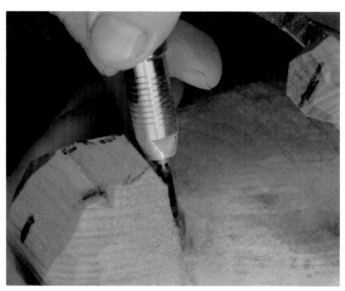

Once the arm is cut down roughly into the shape and size I want it, I switch to the High Tech with the ball shaped burr and begin to round the arm into shape.

Right now Santa is way too bull-necked. Using the same long conical burr, reduce the size of his neck.

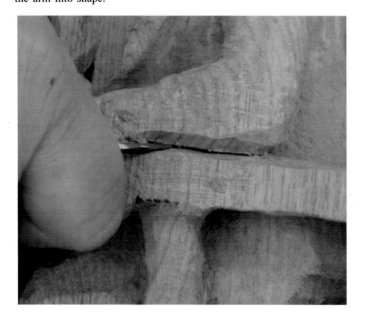

To begin to undercut the left arm I use a sharp knife to get fine lines. I will finish up with the Foredom.

Go all over the figure with the ball shaped burr to add large features (such as the sway in the back) and to round others like Santa's belly. Make the belly round and symmetrical. (In tight places, the conical burr will work best, however.)

Use the narrow, conical burr to separate Santa's backside from the chair back.

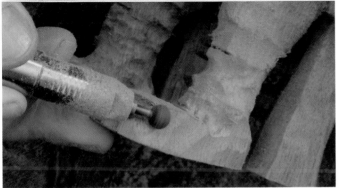

Rounding off the socks and feet at the ankles and the toes.

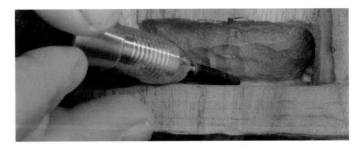

Using the same conical burr, create some separation between the chair's seat and Santa's seat.

Create a band around the bottom of Santa's pants, where they fit in tight like snow pants. Move down a bit and create the top of the sock, where it fits under the pants.

Round off the octagonal edges from the chair legs with the conical burr. You could leave them in place for a rustic look if you wished.

Run the ball shaped burr around the leg in a circle at the joint to create the bulge of the knee cap beneath the pants.

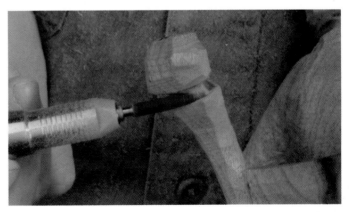

Creating separation between the upper chair leg and the ball at the very tip.

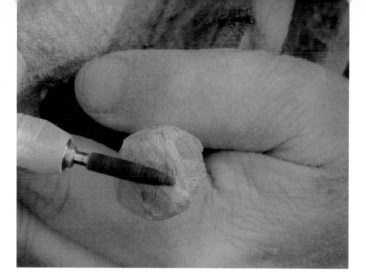

Rounding the ball at the top of the chair.

Like this.

The rounded upper chair leg and ball.

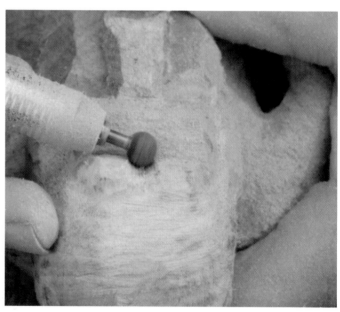

Separate the eyebrows.

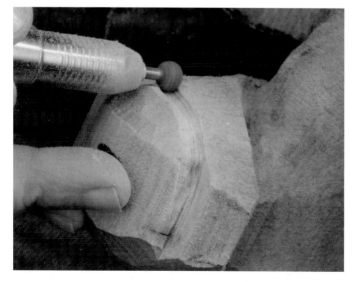

Polishing the head up and creating the separation between the top of Santa's bald head and the fringe of hair he has around the sides using the ball shaped burr in the High Tech.

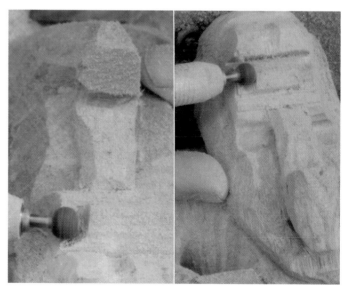

Narrow up the nose some but be careful to leave it wide enough to work on.

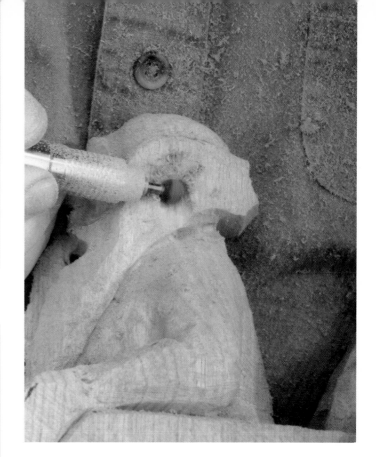

Carving in a place for the ear. The ear goes just behind the centerline of the head. The bottom of the ear will cut off even with the bottom of the nose. Place the ear just behind where you imagine the line of the jaw extends upward. The cut I am making here will become the hollow inside the ear itself.

An ear opening in the hair is in place.

Narrowing down the pipe stem.

Defining the line of the mustache. At this stage burns won't matter. These bits aren't hurt by this. If they become too clogged with wood debris you can burn them clean with torch.

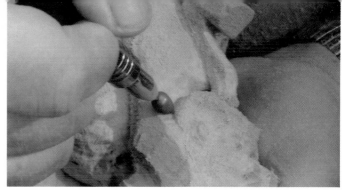

This tear drop shaped conical burr in the High Tech is good for getting into tight places, like below the mustache. It also works well when smoothing out the beard.

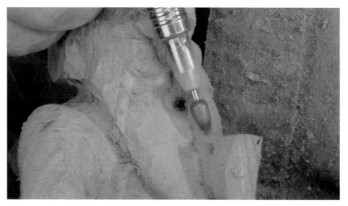

Rounding in around the pipe stem.

Continuing to round the top of the head. I call this "chrome polishing."

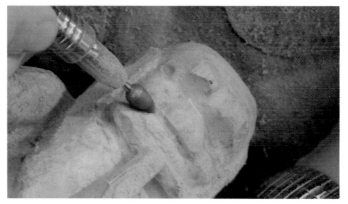

Santa's head is shaping up. A friendly Santa always has an upturned mustache.

Roughing out the flange over the nostril.

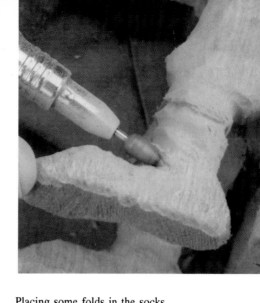

Working around the pipe and starting to leave a lip.

Placing some folds in the socks.

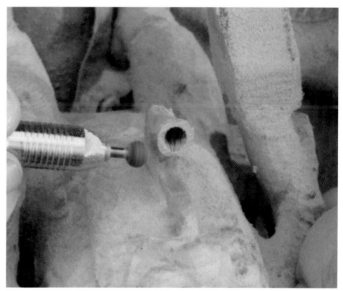

The area of the lower lip is now in place.

Using the ball shaped burr in the High Tech, hollow out the opening in the top of the pipe bowl just a bit.

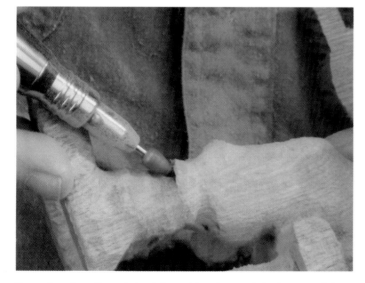

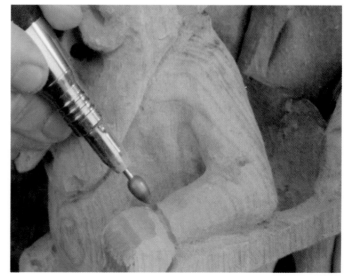

Increasing the effect of the tightened band around the bottom of the pants (with a conical burr in the High Tech) and the line where the bottom of the pants meet the socks.

Carving in the separation of the shirt sleeve with a conical shaped burr in the High Tech.

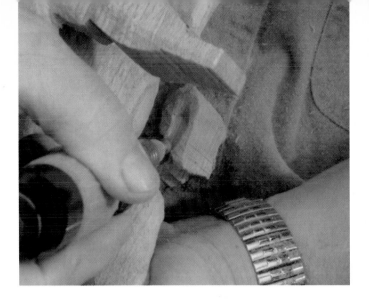

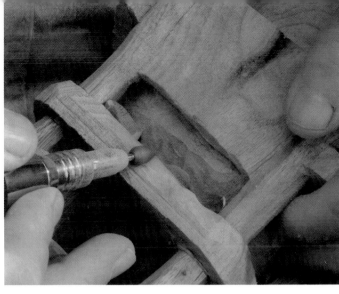

Using the tear drop shaped conical burr, begin to carve in the thumb of the left hand.

Using the High Tech with the tear drop shaped conical burr, smooth down the edges of the chair.

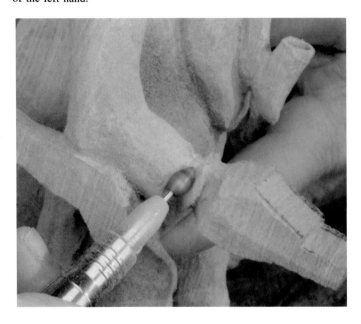

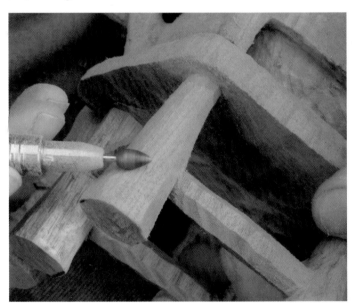

The shirt sleeve on the right arm blouses out just above the end of the sleeve. This can be shown by making a small indentation just behind the end of the shirt cuff.

Narrowing down the chair legs.

Using the power chisel to remove the corners of the chair.

Rounding down the chair rungs.

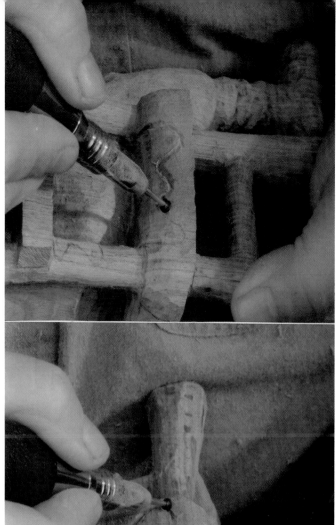

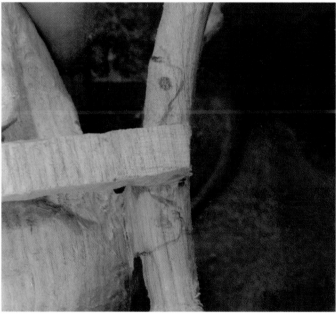

Draw in some upholstery and upholstery tacks along the back and seat of Santa's chair if you wish.

Using a small doughnut shaped disc burr in the High Tech, angle the blade and follow the edge of the tacked down coverings you drew. The angle will remove stock from the chair and give the covering the appearance of being raised up above the level of the wooden chair seat or back.

Could it be reindeer skin? Coverings shown drawn in place on both the seat and back of the chair. Santa's built for comfort, after all; he would never sit in a hard chair.

Continuing to carve in the seat covering. Go ahead and further reduce the wood away from below the seat coverings.

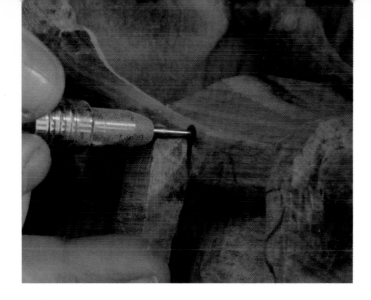

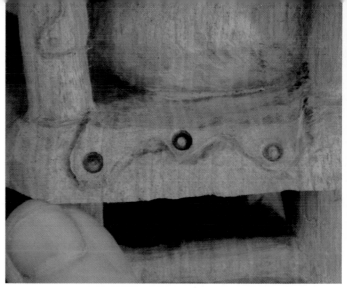

Separating the chair arm from the back a bit. Making it look like it is attached to the back and not a part of it.

Like this.

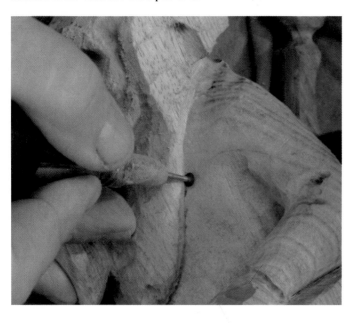

Separating Santa's beard from his chest, again with the small doughnut shaped disc burr in the High Tech.

Or you can use a ball shaped burr in the High Tech to carve in stress marks around the location of the tack heads and then ...

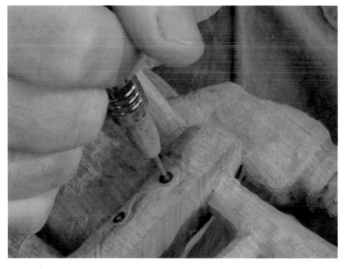

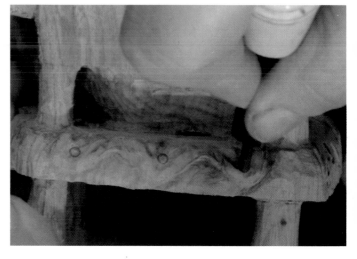

The doughnut shaped disc burr can be used to cut in the tacks holding the seat and chair back coverings in place.

... place in the tack heads with an eye punch from Woodcraft Supply Corp. Always remember that the square shaft eye punches are the best.

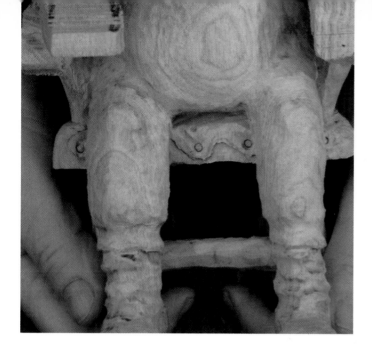

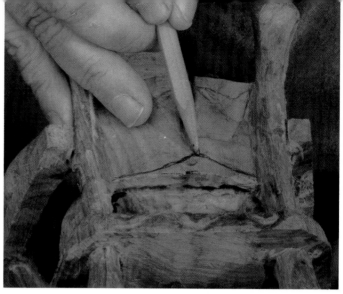

Finish up by carving in the stretched and tacked coverings along the chair back.

Don't forget to carve the covering and tacks in along the front of the chair.

The completed coverings.

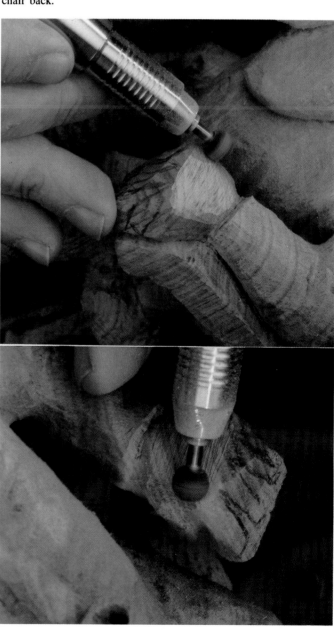

When carving the hand with a ball shaped burr in the High Tech, there are four planes to carve. The back of the hand, ...

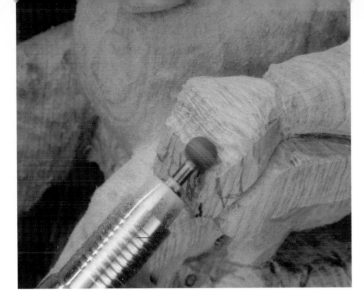

... the knuckles to the first joint, ...

Draw in the fingers in pencil. Separate the fingers using the narrow, conical burr in the High Tech.

... the first to second joint, ...

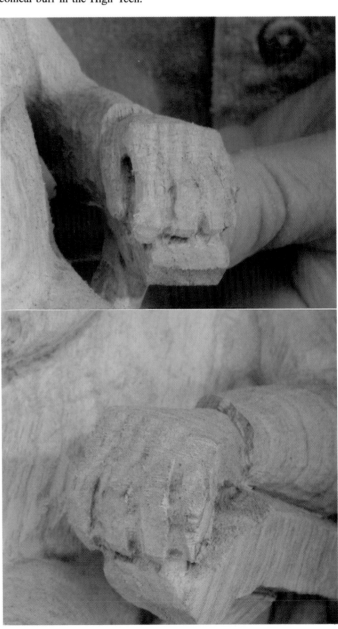

... and the finger tips. Don't forget the thumb while your at it. The ball shaped burr roughs in these planes well.

Like this.

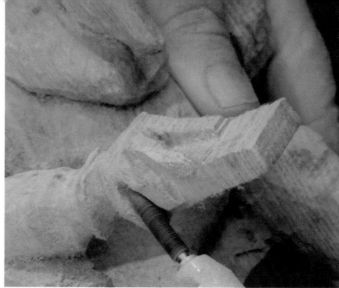

Begin working on the right hand. Start underneath by reducing the stock between the thumb and finger tips using the ball shaped burr in the High Tech.

Separate the fingers with the narrow, conical burr.

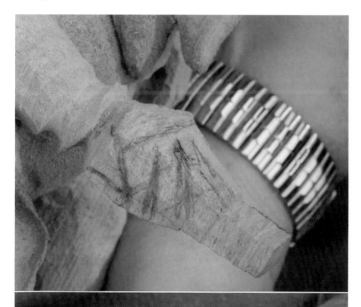

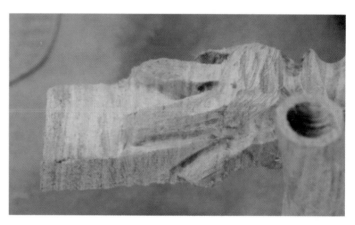

The roughed out hand and remote.

The right hand is drawn in. The index finger is sticking out straight to control the TV remote and the rest of the fingers are curled around the side. Note the angle of the knuckles and joints.

Santa is taking shape.

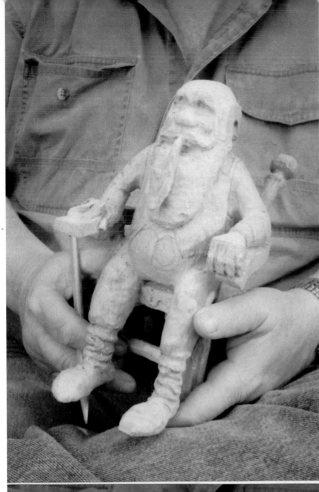

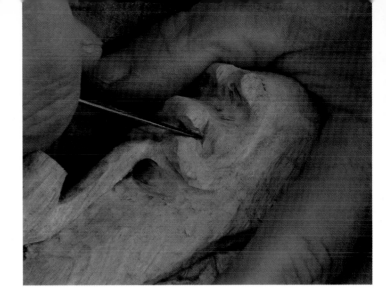

Clean out the lines around the nose with a knife blade.

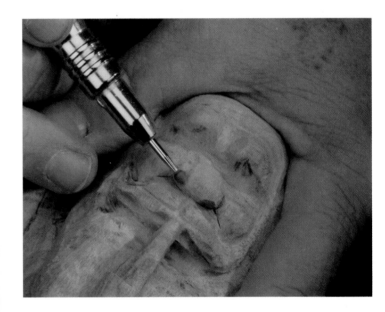

Defining the flanges over the nostrils and the little round ball that comprises the center of the nose using a small egg shaped burr in the High Tech.

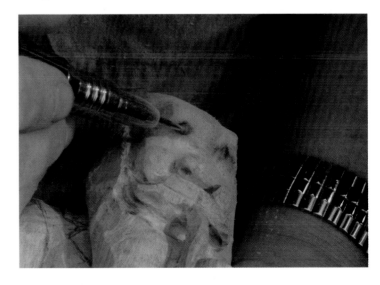

Draw some clothes on Santa in pencil.

Further defining the eye sockets as well.

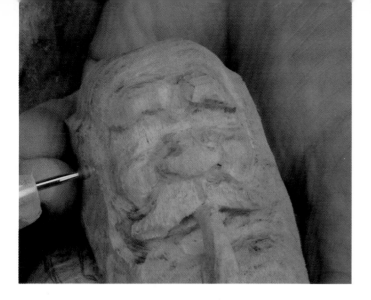

Here is the overall shape of the nose.

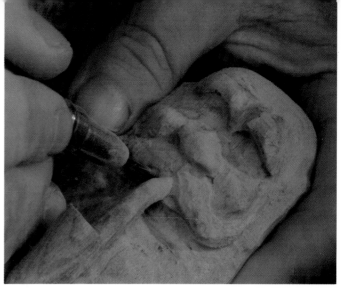

Undercut the wood below the mouth to define the lower lip and separate the sides of the mustache under the nose.

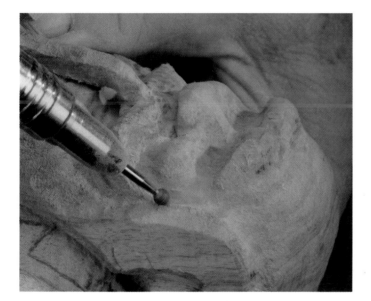

Rounding the cheek over.

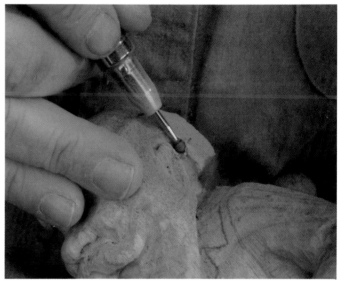

To begin carving the ear with the small egg shaped burr, first place in the curve of the outside of the ear, using the depression you created earlier as the hollow for the center of the ear.

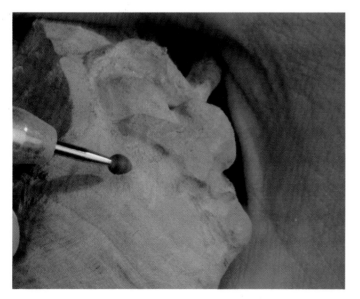

Carve in a line at the base of the eyebrows to raise them above the surrounding surface of the head.

To carve the inside of the ear, place a high and low hole inside the depression of the center of the ear with a small ball shaped burr and
...

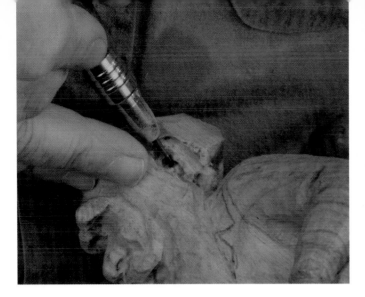

... connect the two with a curing line.

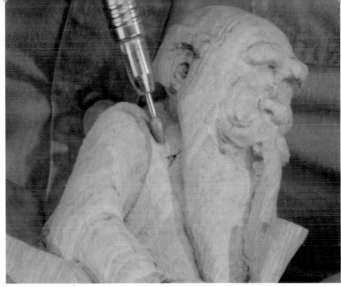

Smooth down the cut lines with the High Tech and a conical shaped burr. This also lowers the wood below the level of raised collars and seams.

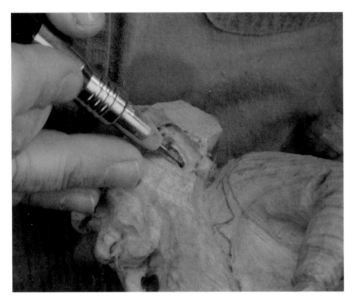

Carve a narrow line along the inner edge of the outer curve of the ear as well if you have room.

Using the doughnut shaped disc burr to smooth out the area where Santa's vest, shirt and pants meet.

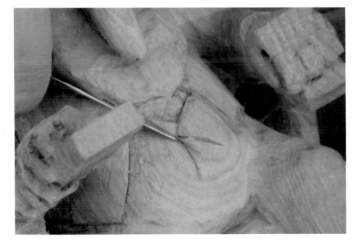

Place a shallow stop cut along the lines of the clothes. Come back to it at a low angle and remove the sliver of wood. This will define the outline of the clothes. I'm using my Case pocket knife again for this particular job. Continue this process around the lines of all of the clothing.

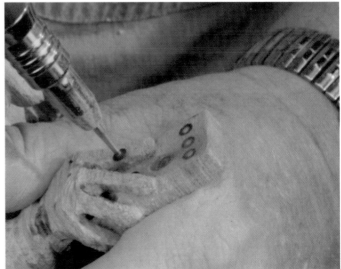

Using the entire round head of this burr also works well when carving in controls on the remote.

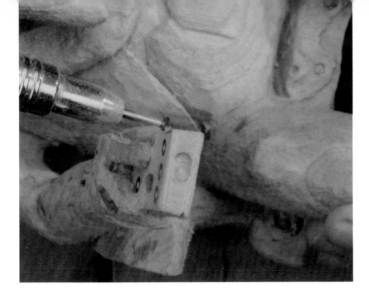

Make the remote as detailed as you like. The edge of the disc shaped burr was also used to carve in the lines around the edge of the remote and the lozenge shaped hollow in front.

Carve in the knuckles, dividing between them with the egg shaped conical burr. Bring the notch up the flat back of the hand a bit to suggest the bones leading back from the knuckles toward the wrist.

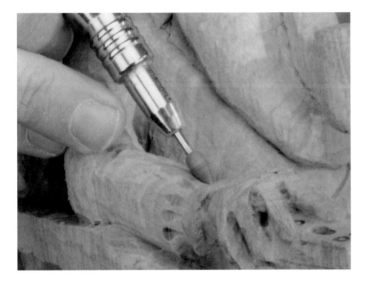

The edge of the egg shaped conical burr may be used to indicate the folds along the edges of the shirt cuffs by laying the edge of the burr along the length of the sleeve with the point facing the cuff.

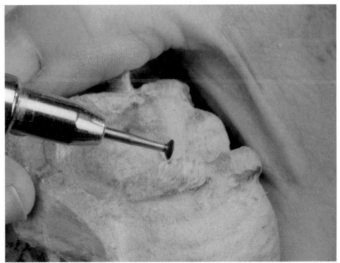

Carve in the hair with a disc shaped burr in the High Tech. I'm starting with the eyebrows.

This burr is also good for placing in wrinkles like these behind the knees.

The eyebrows and mustache hair lines are in place. Remember to make the hair follow the curves of the head. Note the sweep of the hair in the mustache. I am starting on the sideburns now.

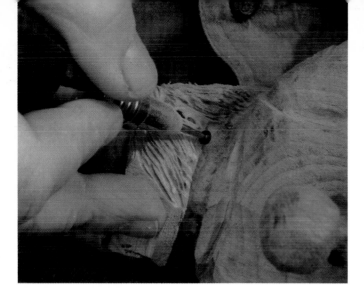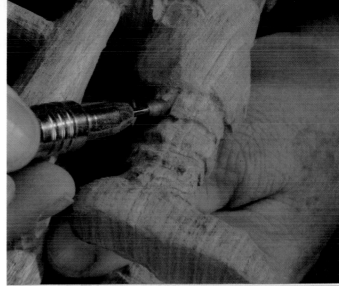

Carving in the hair on the back of the head.

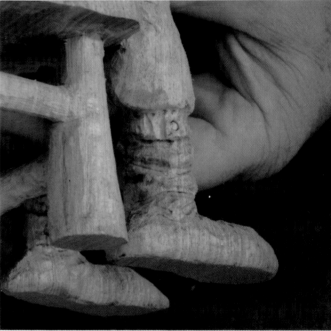

Carving in the hair of the beard, using thin curving lines. Don't worry about getting in all the details now. The rest will be placed after the piece has been sanded to remove the "fuzzies."

I've decided the cuffs of Santa's pants should be held tight with a button. Place a vertical line in the cuff indicating where the two halves meet and use the eye punch to create the button.

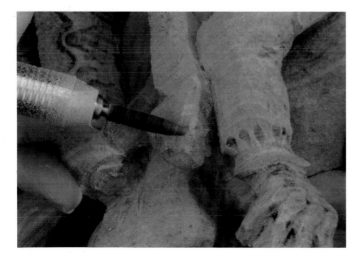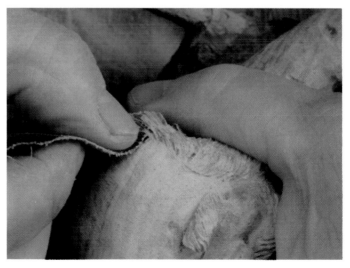

Round off the sharp edges on the arms of the chair for a more finished look. I am using the long narrow conical burr in the High Tech for this job.

Sand the figure to remove the fuzzies. I'm using 220 grit sandpaper and beginning by polishing Santa's "chrome dome."

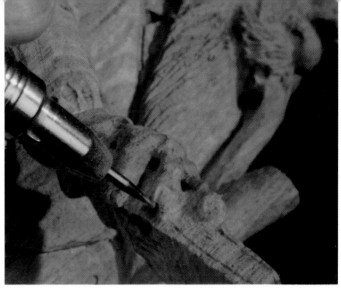

Well, nobody gets everything right the first time. The top of Santa's head is too flat. I'm using the conical burr to round it up some.

Add the fingernails with the smallest ball shaped burr you have.

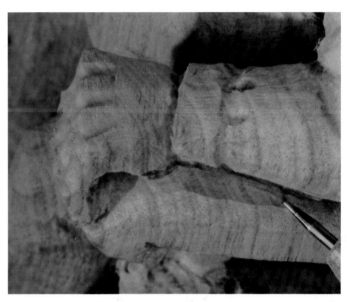

Use the eye punch to put buttons along the front of the pants.

Accentuate the positive ... undercutting between the arm and the chair rest with the smallest ball shaped burr.

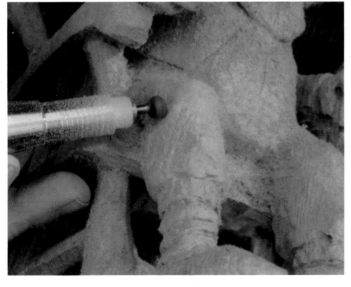

I noticed that this leg was bigger than the other one. I'm narrowing it down with a ball shaped burr on the High Tech.

Like so.

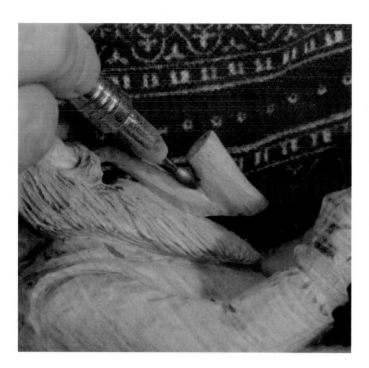

I'm also refining that mouth as I get the stem down.

I'm using an elongated tear drop shaped burr, which gives me more cutting surface to use, to reduce the size of Santa's pipe. Right now it looks like it would be heavy enough to make his front teeth droop.

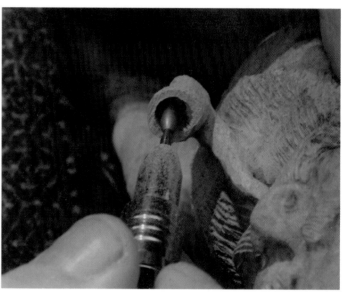

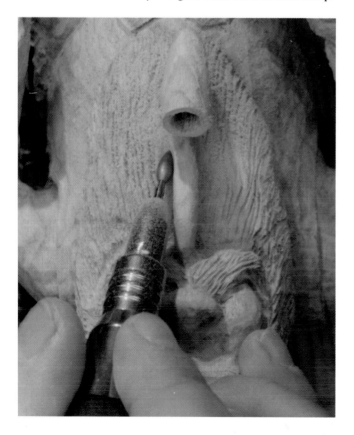

Push in gently with the end of this burr to remove the grill texture from inside the pipe. I want it to look like it has ashes and tobacco inside.

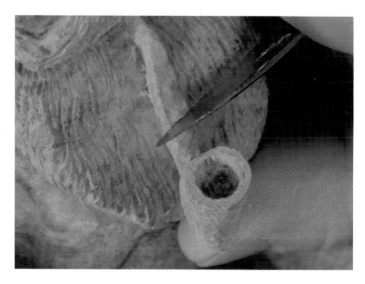

Continuing to reduce the size of the pipe.

Use your knife to carve in a small line separating the stem from the pipe bowl.

Now, before putting in the eyes, give the entire piece a good sanding to get rid of the fuzzies left behind by the burrs. If you sand after putting in the eyes, you will lose most of their detail.

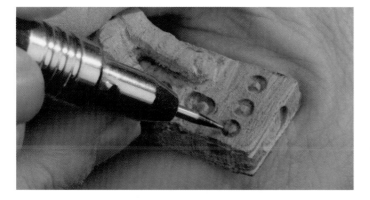

Use the smallest ball shaped burr in the High Tech to remove the burn marks from inside the button controls of the remote (Santa's "surf board").

You can either use a 7/32" eye punch or a pocket knife to create Santa's eyes. I've elected to use my Case knife. First draw in your reference points in pencil. These will give you the rough size and angle of the eyes. As a rule of thumb, you should be able to get five eyes across the head, one from the outside of the head to the outer edge of the eye, another between the inside corners of both eyes and so on. Go ahead and draw in the shape of the eyes, following your guide lines.

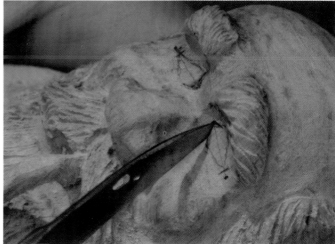

A knife that turns down on the end or one with a very small point is what you will need to get into the corners of the eyes. Carefully cut straight in with the tip of the blade along the upper lid of the eye from the inside corner first.

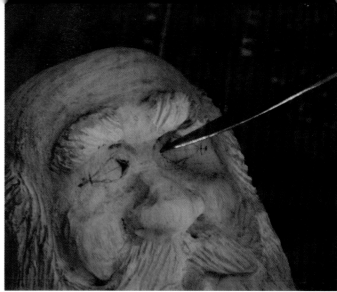

Cut straight in along the lower inside corner of the lid.

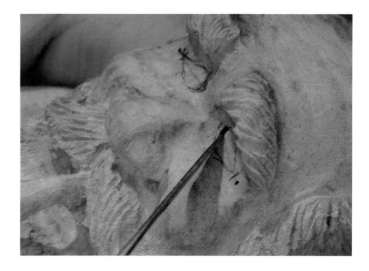

Cut in at an angle into the corner of the eye, into these two stop cuts, creating an inverted pyramid. If the excess triangle of wood doesn't pop right out, follow each step again. Proceed like this on all four corners of the eye. This will begin to round the eyeball as you go.

Now cut in straight with the tip of your blade from cut to cut.

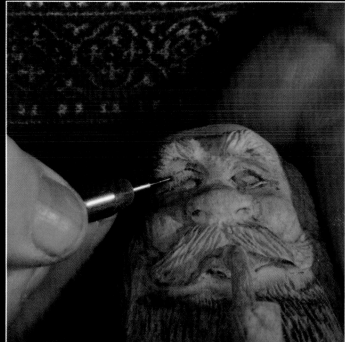

Take that same little ball shaped burr in the High Tech that we've been using and go back and cut in the lids. Get the lids as thin as you can without breaking them off. You don't want them looking too puffy.

Now come back at an angle and remove the excess wood. This will give you the impression of the eyeball being a lot bigger than what is shown and of it going back in under the lids.

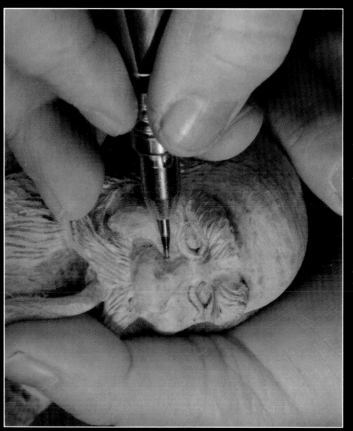

While here, I'm putting a little accent in around the nose.

The carving is finished, awaiting paint or stain.

# A WORD ABOUT PAINTING SANTAS

For wood carving I have been using Winsor and Newton Alkyd tube paints. However, I am slowly switching over from alkaline to oil paints. Alkaline paints are becoming difficult to find and I hear rumors that they will be discontinued. Alkaline and oil paints are compatible together as well. You can paint or stain this figure as you wish. You can also leave it unfinished and let nature do with it what it will. Just keep it clean. I prefer to finish hard woods like this butternut in a natural finish ... although it can be painted. If you're working with bass wood you will probably want to paint it.

The paints are thinned with pure turpentine to a consistency that works with the carving. I mix my paints in glass juice bottles, putting in a bit of paint and adding turpentine. I don't use exact measurements. Instead I use trial and error, adding a bit of paint or a bit of turpentine until I get the thickness I want.

What I look for is a watery mixture, almost like a wash. In this way the turpentine will carry the pigment into the wood, giving the stained look I like. It has always been my theory that if you are going to cover the wood, why use wood in the first place. It should be noted that with white, the concentration of pigment should be a little stronger.

The juice bottles are handy for holding your paints. They are reclosable, easy to shake, and have the added advantage of leaving a concentrated amount of color on the inside of the lid and the sides of the bottle which can be used when more intense color is needed.

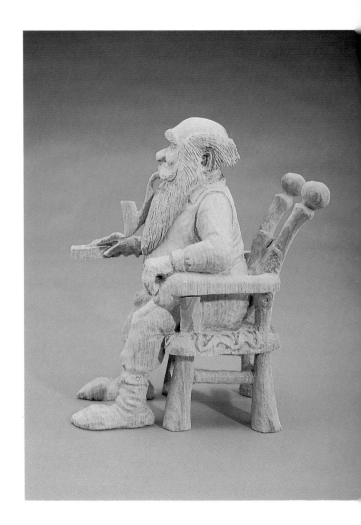

The completed **Surfin' Santa**, carved in butternut.

**T'was the Morning After.** Carved from basswood.

This pattern is 85% of original size.

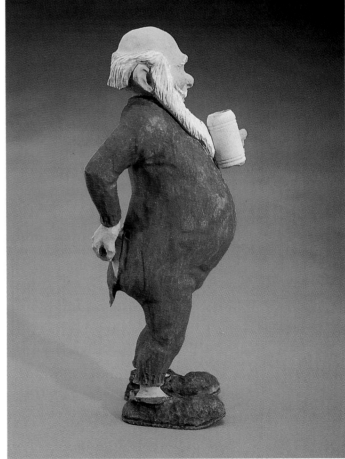

This pattern is 62% of original size.

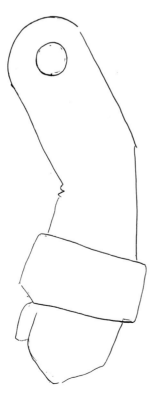

**Hi Kids!** Carved from basswood.

**No, this way is South!** Carved from basswood.

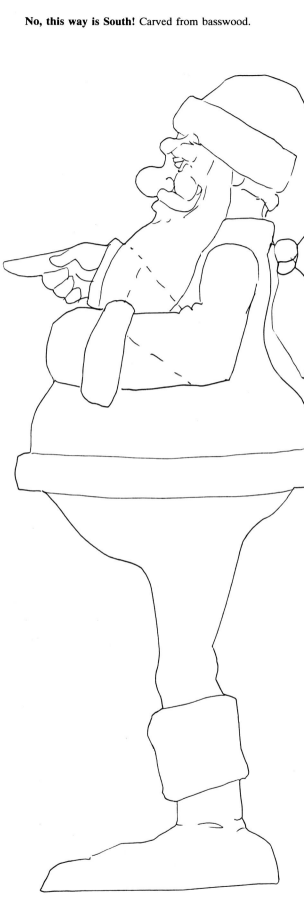

This pattern is 85% of original size.